Contents

EMINEM

Mike Wilson

Published in association with The Basic Skills Agency

Hodder Murray

A MEMBER OF THE HODDER HEADLINE GROUP

The Publishers would like to thank the following for permission to reproduce copyright material:

Photo credits
pp.2, 12, 27 © AP Photo; pp.8, 19 © PA/Empics; p.22 © British Film Institute.

Orders: please contact Bookpoint Ltd, 130 Milton Park, Abingdon, Oxon OX14 4SB. Telephone: (44) 01235 827720. Fax: (44) 01235 400454. Lines are open from 9.00–6.00, Monday to Saturday, with a 24-hour message answering service. Visit our website at www.hoddereducation.co.uk.

© Mike Wilson 2002, 2005
Second Edition. First published in 2002 by
Hodder Murray, a member of the Hodder Headline Group
338 Euston Road
London NW1 3BH

Impression number   10 9 8 7 6 5 4 3 2
Year   2010 2009 2008 2007 2006 2005

Cover photo © Giovanni Canitano/Rex Features
Typeset in 14pt Palatino by SX Composing DTP, Rayleigh, Essex.
Printed in Great Britain by CPI Bath.

A catalogue record for this title is available from the British Library

ISBN-10 0 340 90080 6
ISBN-13 978 0 340 90080 2

Introduction

Is he really that sick?
Is he really that evil?
Is he really that angry?

Or is he a genius MC – the best rapper yet?

Does he really mean all the things he says?
Does he really want to kill his ex-wife?
Does he really hate gay people?
Does he really hate Britney Spears?

There are lots of questions about Eminem.
Lots of opinions, lots of wasted words.
Here, we look at the people in his life.
Friends, family. Enemies.
The people who make him what he is.

They all have something to say about him.
One thing they all agree on:
you either love Eminem, or you hate him.

Eminem: love him or hate him?

1 The Father

Eminem was born on 17 October 1974.
He was named Marshall Mathers III
after his father, Marshall Mathers II.

Six months later,
his father left home.
Eminem has never seen a photo of him.

When he was older,
Marshall tried writing to his dad.
He never got a reply.

Later, when Eminem was rich and famous,
his dad tried to get in touch.

He never got a reply.

2 The Mother

Marshall's mother is called Debbie.
She looked after him on her own
when he was a child.

'Six months was the longest
we ever lived in a house,' he remembers.

In 2001, his mother tried to sue Eminem
for ten million dollars.
It was for all the bad things
he had said about her in his songs.

Eminem said she was white trash.
Always drinking, always on drugs.
Debbie got 10,000 dollars from the court case,
but her lawyers took most of that.

Eminem told her in another song,
'I hope you burn in hell . . .
. . . for the way you treated me!'

3 DeAngelo Bailey

Marshall went to lots of different schools.

He was a skinny little white kid
in the poor, black part of town.
He got picked on a lot by bullies.
One of the bullies was DeAngelo Bailey.

One time, Marshall got hit so hard,
he blacked out, and ended up in hospital.
Eminem told the story in a song.
It was called 'Brain Damage'.

DeAngelo Bailey took Eminem to court
in March 2002.
He was named in the 'Brain Damage' song.
DeAngelo claimed it was cruel and untrue,
and he wanted one million dollars.

He didn't get it.

4 Uncle Ronnie

Marshall never knew his dad.
But he was really close to his Uncle Ronnie.
Ronnie was just a few years older.
He was like a big brother.

Ronnie was into music.
He played the first rap song
that young Marshall Mathers ever heard.
It was 'Reckless', by Ice-T.

Marshall was only nine years old.
But he knew rap music was his life.

Ten years later, Uncle Ronnie killed himself.
Eminem didn't speak for days.
Death and suicide had become
part of his life.

Eminem has a big tattoo on his left arm.
It's there to remind him of his Uncle Ronnie.

5 The Dirty Dozen

When he was 15,
Marshall dropped out of school
and started looking for work.

He worked in kitchens
and he cleaned toilets.
But he knew he wanted to be a rapper.

He started hanging around street corners
with the other rappers.

At first, they all dissed him,
because he was white.
But when they heard him rap,
they knew he was good.
Colour didn't matter.

Eminem performing with a member of D-12.

For the first time,
Eminem made friends.
There was Proof, Swifty, Kon Artis,
Kuniva and Bizarre.
There were six of them, with Eminem.
But they all had an aka
when they were rapping.
It's like they were all two people.
So altogether there were 12.

They called themselves the Dirty Dozen,
or D-12 for short.

The Dirty Dozen made a promise:
if one of them made it big,
he'd remember his friends.

In 2001, when Eminem started his own label,
D-12 was the first act he signed.
He made an album with them.
Devil's Night came out in 2001.

6 Slim Shady

The name 'Eminem' comes from
Marshall Mathers' initials – M and M.
One day, Eminem thought of the name
'Slim Shady'.
He thought of all these words
that rhymed with 'Slim Shady'.
He knew he'd found his aka.

Slim Shady is part of Marshall Mathers.
Slim Shady is inside him, screaming to get out.

Slim Shady is all the things
Marshall Mathers can never be.
He says all the things
Marshall Mathers can never say.

He has all the disgusting, violent ideas.
He's the one full of hate and anger.
Slim Shady is the crazy one.
He's the one with the sick sense of humour.

7 Dr Dre

When Eminem was a boy,
he'd listen to Dr Dre's band, NWA.
They were heroes to him.

Now here he was,
working in the studio with Dr Dre,
rapping together on tracks like 'Guilty Conscience'.

In a few short years,
Eminem's dream had come true.

It was January 1998,
and Marshall Mathers was 23.

Back in 1997, Dr Dre heard a demo tape.
It was the *Slim Shady EP*.
Someone asked him
what he thought of the rapper.

Dre said, 'Find him. Now.'

Dr Dre was Eminem's hero, when he was a boy.

When Dr Dre first heard Eminem,
he didn't know he was white.
When Dre found out,
it didn't change a thing.

'If you're dope, you're dope,'
was all the man said.
He meant, 'If you're good, you're good.'

Eminem got street cred,
working with the great Dr Dre.
Dre gave him a start in the business,
and a fan base for his music.

Eminem learned a lot from Dre.
He says simply,
'Dre is the best producer of all time.'

Dre says,
'Someone like Eminem is rare.
I haven't made many friends
in this rap game.
But Eminem is one.'

8 Kim

'I don't hate women,' says Eminem.
'They just make me mad sometimes.'

He's thinking of Kim, his ex-wife.
They started dating when he was 16.
Kim was 14 when she moved in
with Marshall and his mum.
They were always fighting, splitting up,
always getting back together.

They had a baby. They got married.
It didn't stop the fights.

The anger came out in Eminem's music.
He'd rap about killing his wife
in songs like 'Kim', 'Just The Two Of Us'
and '97 Bonnie and Clyde'.

In the songs, Kim was always getting stabbed
and left to die.

There is a lot of violence against women
in Eminem's songs and videos.
His anger – at his mum, his wife
and his early life – is there for all to see.

It was all too much for Kim Mathers.
In July 2000,
she tried to kill herself.

In August, Eminem filed for divorce.
They'd been married for 14 months.

Kim tried to sue him for mental cruelty.
She wanted ten million dollars.
They settled out of court.

In 2002, Eminem said,
'I won't get married again.
Once was enough.
I'd rather be stuck on a plane with *NSYNC
than get married again!'

9 John Guerra

There are two sides to every story.

This is how Eminem tells it:
He found his wife cheating on him
with another man.
He got mad and wanted to kill them both.

End of story.

This is how John Guerra tells the story:
It was June 2000.
He was out drinking with some friends.
One of them was Kim Mathers.

When they said goodbye, in the car park,
Kim gave him a kiss on the cheek.

'She's a friendly person!' said John Guerra.
'There was nothing funny going on!'

Next thing,
he heard, 'Gun! Gun! Gun!'
Eminem knocked John Guerra
to the ground with a gun.
Eminem stood over him.
He said he would kill Guerra,
then he'd kill his ex-wife.

They managed to calm him down.

Eminem ended up in court again
for having a gun without a licence.

In April 2001,
Eminem walked free.
He got just two years' probation,
as it was his first offence.

Eminem cleaned up his act after that.
It was part of the deal
with the two years' probation:
no drink, no drugs, no guns,
no more fights.

10 Elton John

Many people hate the violence
in Eminem's songs.
They hate what he says about gay people.

But if Eminem hates gay people,
why did he work with Elton John?
And why did Elton work with him?

At the Grammy Awards in 2001,
Elton and Eminem sang 'Stan' together.
Elton put his arm round Eminem.

Eminem with Elton John at the 2001 Grammy Awards.

Elton said,
'Eminem's music is hardcore.
It's clever, and funny.
It's poetry.
I've worked with Eminem
and he does not hate gays!'

 'I didn't know about his personal life,'
Eminem said. 'I didn't really care.'
So maybe hating gays is just part of the act.

11 Rabbit

His real name is Jimmy Smith Junior.
But everyone calls him Rabbit.
Eminem plays the part of Rabbit
in the 2002 movie *8 Mile*.

8 Mile is a part of Detroit.
It's the name of the road
that splits the poor black areas
from the poor white areas.

Rabbit works in a car factory.
He's poor, white trash.
He's mixed up and angry. And shy.
He's got a no-hope mother,
and a no-hope girlfriend.
His only hope of escape
is making it as a rap artist.

Eminem didn't need acting lessons
to play the part of Rabbit.

Eminem as Rabbit in *8 Mile*.

But Eminem could act.
He looked good on screen.
He looked moody, and mean.
We even got to see him smile –
just a little!

The movie's producer said,
'I always knew Eminem could act.
Then when he came on set,
I couldn't take my eyes off him.'

Eminem said, 'We took some things
that happened in my life.
And we twisted them a little bit.
We added some things,
and took out some things.'

So Marshall Mathers had another aka.
First Slim Shady,
and then Jimmy Smith Junior,
were trying to make sense of his life.

Eminem got some respect as an actor.
And *8 Mile* got respect
as one of the best movies about rap.

12 Hailie Jade

Eminem says he'll never fall in love again.
But there's one person he'll always love:
his daughter Hailie Jade.

'I'd never write a song
about how much I love her,' he has said.
'I don't want to get all mushy!'

But then he did just that.
'Hailie's Song' was on his 2002 CD,
The Eminem Show.
Eminem actually sings on the song.
He tells her she's the only lady he loves.
'If you ever need anything,
Daddy will be right there . . .'

Only a few years before,
when Hailie was just three years old,
he'd used her voice on '97 Bonnie and Clyde'.
The song about killing her mother . . .

'Yeah,' said Eminem.
'When I did that,
I wanted to hit back at Kim.
She wasn't letting me see my little girl.
She was using Hailie as a weapon!

'I'll explain all that to Hailie
when she's old enough . . .'

In 2001, Eminem won a Grammy Award.
The Marshall Mathers LP won Best Rap Album
and went on to sell eight million copies.

In his speech, Eminem told Hailie Jade,
'Daddy loves you . . .'

He spends all the time he can with Hailie.
He takes her to school, and picks her up.
'We watch TV,' he says. 'Typical stuff.'
'And when I'm around Hailie,' he says,
'I limit the swear words!'

What is happening to the hard man of rap?

13 Eminem

The last words go to Eminem himself.
Here are some of the things
he has said about himself.

'Sometimes I mean what I say.
Sometimes I am playing a part.
It's up to you to tell which is which.

'Anybody with half a brain
can tell when I'm joking
and when I'm serious.

'Young people have a sense of humour.
They can tell right from wrong.
Kids are a lot smarter than we think.

'Do you think I worry
in case you're offended?
I've been offended all my life!'

Eminem isn't scared of offending.

'If you don't like my music,
it's not my problem.
Nobody's forcing you to listen.
Nobody tied you up
and made you listen!

'Just cos I say, "Go and rape a girl",
it doesn't mean go and do it.
I'm just saying, it goes on in the world.

'I just say whatever I want,
to whoever I want,
whenever I want,
wherever I want,
however I want.

'That's how I am.
I think of something, I say it.

'Maybe I'll regret it later.
Maybe I won't.'